"I loved the prairie by instinct

as a great simplicity, the trees and flowers,

the sky itself, thrilling by contrast."–1931

FRANK LLOYD WRIGHT

AND THE

PRAIRIE

MELANIE BIRK

The Frank Lloyd Wright Home and Studio Foundation

UNIVERSE

This book is published on the

occasion of the centennial of Frank Lloyd Wright's

studio in Oak Park, Illinois.

ACKNOWLEDGMENTS

I would like to thank the following staff members at the Frank Lloyd Wright Home and Studio Foundation for their assistance in producing this book: Joan Mercuri, executive director; Cheryl Bachand, curator of collections; Fran Martone, curatorial assistant; Erin McAfee, assistant to the curator; Jean Guarino, public relations director; and Gay Anderson, merchandise director. I also thank Michael Houlahan of Hedrich Blessing for his generosity with the photography of the Foundation's museum sites.

—*Melanie Birk*

YE'VE LEFT A GLIMMER STILL TO CHEER
THE MAN–THE ARTIFEX
THAT HOLDS IN SPITE O' KNOCKS AND SCALE
O' FRICTION WASTE AN' SLIP.
AN' BY THAT LIGHT – NOW MARK MY WORD –
WE'LL BUILD THE PERFECT SHIP.

Front cover: Frederick C. Robie House (1909–1910).
Back cover and page 2: Frank Lloyd Wright, date unknown.
Casing: Design based on c. 1977 restoration drawing of ceiling grille
in dining room of Frank Lloyd Wright's home, Oak Park, Illinois
(original in wood, c. 1895).
Endpages: Design based on c. 1977 restoration drawing of ceiling
grille in Wright's Oak Park home (original in wood, c. 1895).
Page 5: Drafting room, Wright's Oak Park studio.
Page 7: Art glass entry, Susan Lawrence Dana House (1902–1904).
Page 8: Frank Lloyd Wright, c. 1904.

First published in the United States of America in 1998
by UNIVERSE PUBLISHING
A Division of Rizzoli International Publications, Inc.
300 Park Avenue South
New York, NY 10010

Copyright © 1998 The Frank Lloyd Wright
Home and Studio Foundation

98 99 00 01 / 10 9 8 7 6 5 4 3 2 1

Printed in Singapore

Library of Congress Cataloging-in-Publication Data

Birk, Melanie
        Frank Lloyd Wright and the Prairie / Melanie Birk, the
Frank Lloyd Wright Home and Studio Foundation.
                        p.   cm.
        Includes bibliographical references.
        ISBN 0-7893-0140-7 (hc)
        1. Wright, Frank Lloyd, 1867–1959—Criticism and inter-
pretation.   2. Prairie school (Architecture)—Illinois—Oak Park
Region.   3. Architecture, Domestic—Illinois—Oak Park
Region.   I. Frank Lloyd Wright Home and Studio Foundation.
II. Title.
NA737.W7B53   1998
720'.92—dc21
                                                97-51560
                                                CIP

FRANK LLOYD WRIGHT began his remarkable, seventy-year career with the intensity and imagination of a true revolutionary. Starting with the design of his own home in 1889 in Oak Park, Illinois, Wright embarked upon a period of extraordinary energy and focus that spanned two decades and changed the course of American residential architecture. Today, the largest single collection of Wright's work can be found within a few square miles of his Oak Park home and adjacent studio. This legacy was inspired by the architect's profound and personal love of the vast, virgin grasslands that, at the time, still surrounded the Chicago area.

Entrance to Wright's Oak Park studio.

Wright cherished the prairie of the American Midwest not only as a physical place but also as a metaphor for his vision of the American spirit—courageous, independent, and practical. As his work developed, the houses he built for this landscape became more and more reflective of their natural and cultural setting. Bearing his bold, signature style, these buildings have left an indelible mark on America, transforming the quiet sister suburbs of Oak Park and River Forest, Illinois, into architectural meccas. Pictured on the following pages, these unconventional buildings, and others designed in his Oak Park studio, convey the fervent creativity of Wright's early career and offer a site-by-site showcase of his first major contribution to American design: the Prairie House.

Undeniably American, Frank Lloyd Wright owed much of his inspiration to the landscape and ideals of the Midwest. As a young architect, he began to challenge the classical, Beaux-Arts tradition and to search for a new, indigenous form of building that embodied the "peace of the prairie."[1] The result of this search, which evolved over a twenty-year period

Plant study sketched by Wright and Catherine Tobin, c. 1889, graphite on construction paper, 13 7/8 × 10 inches.

and culminated in the construction of the Frederick C. Robie House, was the remaking of the American home. Along with a group of talented architects, most of whom worked in his Oak Park studio, Wright developed a unique style that, in its emphatic, horizontal lines and open flowing spaces, celebrated the Midwestern landscape, combining utility and beauty and emphasizing natural materials—an altogether new genre that came to be known as the Prairie Style.

Wright's relationship with the prairie began when he was a young boy growing up in rural Spring Green, Wisconsin. His family, many of whom were farmers and devout Unitarians, cultivated in him a deep appreciation for the land and for nature. In his autobiography, Wright described the "virgin American soil" his Welsh ancestors came to inhabit.[2] He wrote extensively about the beauty of the Wisconsin landscape and its ability to nurture his artistic vision, describing it in poetic terms: "A light blanket of snow fresh-fallen over sloping fields, gleaming in the morning sun. Clusters of pod-topped weeds woven of bronze here and there sprinkling the spotless expanse of white. Dark sprays of slender metallic straight lines, tipped with quivering dots. Pattern to the eye of the sun, as the sun spread delicate network of more pattern in blue shadows on the white beneath."[3]

When Wright left Wisconsin for Chicago at age nineteen to practice architecture, his love of the prairie remained strong. After a brief residence in Chicago, he chose to settle in suburban Oak Park, believing that a semi-rural rather than an urban setting would be more conducive to creativity. He adorned his home with prairie weeds and even designed a copper "weed holder." Under the tutelage of his employer and mentor Louis Sullivan—who also defined his architecture by using natural motifs for inspiration and ornamentation—Wright deepened his fondness for the tranquility, simplicity, and expanse of the plains. He incorporated these qualities in his buildings through carefully considered methods and materials, beginning his practice of organic architecture—a term Wright applied to thoughtful, unified design that reflected "the harmonious order we call nature."[4]

Indeed, in Wright's own Oak Park home, built in 1889 for his bride, Catherine Tobin, the earthen colors and natural materials he chose were meant to evoke an air of serenity. The predominant use of geometric shapes, repeated in millwork, art glass, furnishings, and fixtures, conveyed simplicity and a sense of order. Ribbons of casement windows, painted murals, and wide openings between rooms created an array of interconnected interior and exterior vistas. In this building, despite its Shingle-Style façade, Wright planted the seeds of Prairie-Style architecture,

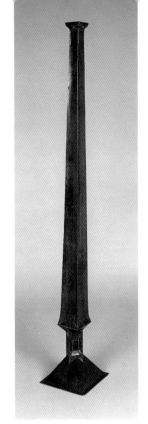

Wright-designed weed holder, c. 1890–1900, copper, 5 × 5 × 28½ inches.

using it as a design laboratory in which to test new ideas. Many of his trademarks can be seen here in their infancy: patterned ceiling grilles, simple built-in furniture, geometrically applied wood trim, fireplace alcoves, bands of windows or "light screens," and the incorporation of decorative arts such as murals, sculptures, and art glass featuring abstracted plant forms.

After leaving the firm of Adler and Sullivan in 1893, Wright began to expand his

Fireplace alcove, or "inglenook," Wright's Oak Park home.

Prairie-Style vocabulary in an independent practice. The first project to earn him recognition was the William Winslow House (1893), a massive, self-contained rectangle with notably flat surfaces and a broad, hipped roof that reflected the horizontality of the prairie. Despite the façade's classical symmetry, the building is a clear predecessor of the mature Prairie Style. Frank Lloyd Wright scholar Grant Manson called the Winslow House "another of the miracles of Wright's career," noting that it was without precedent in the world of architecture.[5] Its weighted brick construction, its basic, geometric form, and its heavy massing visually anchored the house to the ground, symbolizing what Wright saw as the strength and stability of Midwestern culture. For although the prairie landscape was important to Wright, so, too, were such Midwestern ideals as sincerity, fortitude, and integrity —characteristics that Wright aspired to embody in his work.

"Buildings like people must first be sincere,"[6] he wrote in 1908, referring to his belief that a building's design should respond to its setting and to the needs of its owners, rather than to the popularity of a certain mode. Honesty in architecture also meant that a building's exterior form should reflect its interior space—an unfamiliar notion in the Victorian era. "Human use and comfort should have intimate possession of every interior . . . should be felt in every exterior," he wrote in his autobiography.[7]

Wright conveyed a sense of permanence in his houses by using sturdy materials, heavy volumes, and wide, anchoring chimneys. Inside, central hearths and the copious use of wood created an air of strength and vigor. He gave form to the principle of integrity by making his buildings unified and complete unto themselves, likening his structures to growing plants

William H. Winslow House (1893), River Forest, Illinois

and describing them as "organic." His concept of the total environment led Wright to design not only the structure, but also complementary furnishings, fixtures, and decorative objects. Integrity, he said, is the quality that makes a building timeless, placing it beyond the reaches of fashion.

In 1896, in another venture for client William Winslow, who printed and published books from his home, Wright illustrated a book by William Gannett titled *The House Beautiful*. He created drawings inspired by nature and took photographs of prairie plants for the publication, which idealized artistic homes and described Wright's own Oak Park residence. The "House Beautiful" was a concept that developed within the Arts and Crafts tradition—a design movement that had its roots in England and championed simplicity and common sense as its principal ideals. The Midwest was a locus of early Arts and Crafts activity

Wright (far right, seated) with family outside his Oak Park home, c. 1890.

in the United States, and Wright became actively involved in the 1890s, serving as a founding member of the Chicago Arts and Crafts Society. However, while the movement's promotion of simple, functional design influenced Wright, he disagreed with its sole reliance on handcraft; by 1901, he was espousing the virtues of mechanization in a famous address, "The Art and Craft of the Machine."

In 1898, in an effort to bring his work and growing family of six children closer together, Wright built an architectural studio adjacent to his Oak Park home. In realizing Louis Sullivan's axiom, "form follows function," Wright designed his own studio so that its unusual exterior shapes were direct expressions of the spaces within. The square base and upper octagonal drum of the drafting room to the east were balanced by the smaller octagonal form of the library to the west. Linking these two spaces was a skylit reception hall and a loggia crowned by two sculptures of crouching male figures known as "the Boulders."

With its theatrical shapes and sculptures, this studio puzzled neighbors but attracted a small group of young, gifted architects, artisans, and draftsmen. Among the most accomplished of Wright's early protégés were Barry Byrne, William Drummond, George Grant Elmslie, Walter Burley Griffin, Marion Mahony, John Van Bergen, and Charles E. White, Jr. Many of these architects, who worked in the studio for various periods between 1898 and 1909, are credited with important contributions to Wright's work and to the movement that came to be known as the Prairie School. Several of them later distinguished themselves in successful independent practices and partnerships. Other key collaborators included sculptor Richard Bock, artist Orlando Giannini, and furniture and interior designer George Mann Niedecken.

Working in the studio's light-filled drafting room, Wright and his colleagues rebelled against the architectural establishment and shaped an original, distinctly American approach to domestic design. Wright said of Victorian architecture: "Dwellings of that period were cut up, advisedly and completely, with the grim determination that should go with any 'cutting' process. The 'interi-

"The Boulders," Richard Bock sculpture outside Wright's Oak Park studio, painted plaster.

ors' consisted of boxes beside boxes or inside boxes, called rooms."[8] Wright opened up the compartmentalized Victorian floor plan, destroying the "box" by dramatically varying ceiling heights, contrasting open and compressed spaces, and dissolving corners through the use of abutting windows. His own studio featured an octagonal library, a low, dimly lit reception hall, and a soaring, two-story drafting room with a suspended balcony. The studio's artisans worked on the balcony, executing designs for art glass or decorative objects, overlooking the architects below who wore "flowing ties and smocks suitable to the realm."[9]

As the birthplace of the Prairie School of architecture, the studio served as an advertisement for unconventional design. Its irreverent appearance attracted its share of adventurous clients, who in turn enabled Wright and his co-workers to eschew traditional styles and

Ward W. Willits House (1901), Highland Park, Illinois.

experiment with new forms, materials, and technologies. Most of Wright's early clients were independent, self-made men who ran businesses in downtown Chicago. Many were entrepreneurs who respected Wright's penchant for innovation and who, in numerous cases, held common interests with the architect: Frederick Robie shared Wright's fascination with the automobile; Ward Willits was a connoisseur of Japanese art and culture; and William Winslow shared Wright's passion for books. Oak Park was also home to a large Unitarian congregation, which attracted its share of liberal members—including Wright and his family—and provided a stream of clients. In fact, the Oak Park congregation became one of Wright's most important clients when, in 1905, he designed for it his celebrated concrete structure, Unity Temple.

With each commission came an opportunity for Wright to refine his vision of the ideal American home. The Ward Willits Residence (1901), constructed in nearby Highland Park, has become known as the first great Prairie House and a milestone in the architect's early career. Here, Wright increased the complexity of the rectangular Winslow House plan, giving the residence two projecting wings that embraced the suburban site, like outstretched arms, and mirrored the flat terrain. Dark wood banding underlined the horizontal profile. Inside, Wright broke down the limitation of rectangular rooms even further, using partial walls and window groupings to compose views and simulate the effect of movable, Japanese screens. He created a warm, intimate environment within the expansive residence by interweaving rich, unadorned woods, irridescent glass, and autumnal hues.

The design of the Willits House resembled the plan put forth in "A Home in a Prairie Town," submitted by Wright and published in the *Ladies Home Journal* in 1901. Adapted in endless variations for many Prairie houses, this design combined living and dining areas into a single flowing space and introduced the cruciform plan. Most of Wright's Prairie Style plans featured a centrally located fireplace, or inglenook, with rooms radiating outward in the shape of a cross or pinwheel. Wright said, "It comforted me to see the fire burning deep in the solid masonry of the house itself."[10]

Entrance, Frank W. Thomas House (1901–1902), Oak Park, Illinois.

Shortly after the Willits House, in a period of concentrated energy and productivity, Wright designed a series of homes that now form the core of the Prairie School. In Oak Park, just down the street from his own home and studio, stand two of the most significant examples: the Frank Thomas (1901–1902) and Arthur Heurtley (1902) Houses. These buildings epitomized the early Prairie House, with generous hipped roofs and arched entries reminiscent of Louis Sullivan's work. Their hidden front doors became a characteristic trait of the Prairie Style, encouraging visitors to embark on what Wright called "a path of discovery." To enter the Thomas house, one first passed through an archway, then ascended two concealed flights of stairs, and finally located the art glass front door among a row of identical panels—a

Edward R. Hills Residence (1906), Oak Park, Illinois.

path that Wright said heightened a visitor's awareness and appreciation of his environment.

Among Wright's other early houses in Oak Park were the William Fricke (1901) and William E. Martin (1902) Residences. Essentially Prairie houses with vertical blocks or towers, these buildings illustrated Wright's effort to reconcile the style's horizontal emphasis with a three-story plan. Nearby, Wright designed the Peter Beachy (1906) and the Edward Hills (1906) Houses in Oak Park. Their gabled roofs with deep, flared eaves pronounced the influence of Japanese design on the Prairie School—an influence that also manifested itself in modular floor plans and the aesthetic of simplicity. Wright said he learned to admire "the elimination of the insignificant" from his study of Japanese woodblock prints, which he avidly collected.[11] He traveled to Japan for the first time in 1905 with his wife Catherine Tobin Wright and with clients Mr. and Mrs. Ward Willits, documenting his travels through photographs and writings. Wright became deeply influenced by traditional Japanese spatial arrangements and by the harmony that existed between ancient Japanese buildings and nature.

Probably the most elaborate of Wright's Prairie houses was the Susan Dana Residence (1902) in Springfield, Illinois. His heiress client, Susan Lawrence Dana, gave him free rein and ample funds to create a truly extraordinary residence in the heart of the prairie, with every detail reflecting the architect's hand. The first comprehensive design of a total environment, the house featured a collection of Wright-designed decorative arts inspired by the home's natural setting: delicate light fixtures suggestive of butterflies; 250 geometrically patterned art glass windows, doors, and skylights, many based on the native sumac plant; and more than 100 pieces of white oak furniture. A golden brick exterior with a low center of gravity made the building appear to emerge from the earth—a feat Wright often accomplished in his practice of organic architecture.

Art glass entry, Susan Lawrence Dana House (1902), Springfield, Illinois.

Wright was especially fond of the forceful contrast between the flat prairie terrain and the Midwestern sky. A master of drama, he recaptured this effect by endowing his homes with long, projecting cantilevers—elements that mimicked the sharp horizon of the plains. In some Prairie houses, Wright even specified a flat rather than a hipped roof to underscore this effect. Always testing the limits of innovation, he began to extend the cantilevered roof or porch until it seemed to defy gravity, experimenting in projects like the Mrs. Thomas Gale House (1909) in Oak Park. The composition of this house—a sculpture comprised of cubic forms and crisp, intersecting planes—has prompted many to call it a precursor of Wright's 1930s landmark house, Fallingwater.

Frederick C. Robie House (1909–1910), Chicago, Illinois.

Although all of Wright's Prairie houses share common elements, the Prairie Style was not a static formula, but rather an imaginative vision that evolved over time, climaxing in the building of the Frederick C. Robie House (1909–1910) in Chicago. Regarded as the quintessential Prairie House, and certainly his most influential, this residence synthesized many refined ideas about organic design into a single, harmonious structure. Here, in an essay on concrete, wood, glass, and brick, the architect eliminated the wall as a visual barrier or means of support, allowing space to flow freely under a sheltering roof. He dissolved the boundaries between the interior and exterior through the use of window screens and projecting terraces. Outside, he perfected the cantilever with vivid results; so skilled did Wright become at streamlining his design that many compared the Robie House to a modern steamship. Yet, the structure was rooted firmly to the ground by its central chimney core, evoking a sense of familial security and solidity.

"Architecture is the scientific art of making structure express ideas," Wright wrote, and this statement was certainly true of the Prairie houses.[12] Often sited in suburban and sometimes urban locations, as was the Robie House, these structures were not necessarily on the prairie, but rather *about* the prairie and its place in the American cultural landscape. They reflected Wright's conception of Midwestern culture, symbolized by the prairie, and its uncomplicated devotion to individuality, simplicity, and strength. But for all the ideas Wright sought to express in this early work, he was most interested in dramatizing the single, primitive idea of shelter. And no building accomplished this more effectively than the Robie House, with its series of elongated, flat planes that seemed to hover above and protect the private sanctum below. With this building—which the architect himself characterized as "the cornerstone of modern architecture"—Wright's vision of the Prairie Style was fully realized.

Wright left Oak Park for Europe in 1909, celebrating his accomplishments with the publication of the "Wasmuth Portfolio," a German, two-volume retrospective featuring one-hundred plates of his Prairie School work. Many attribute the early influence of Wright's architecture in Europe to the appearance of this publication. In the introduction, Wright salutes the Midwest and the mythic image of the American pioneer, his independence and freedom from the chains of tradition: "The real American spirit, capable of judging an issue for itself upon its merits, lies in the West and Middle West, where breadth of view, independent thought, and a tendency to take common sense into the realm of art, as in life, are more characteristic." Wright admired this American spirit and gave it a tangible, enduring form in his buildings of the Prairie School; he adds, "In America each man has a peculiar, inalienable right to live in his own house in his own way. He is a pioneer in every right sense of the word."[13]

The buildings illustrated in these pages reflect the evolution of the Prairie House and chronicle the search by Wright and his colleagues for an ideal, authentically American dwelling inspired by nature, shaped by human needs, and unified by a system of thoughtfully developed design principles. Constructed about 100 years ago, these buildings appear remarkably contemporary today, continuing to fulfill their roles as active family centers, to influence the design of modern homes, and to serve as models of architectural achievement in their communities.

— MELANIE BIRK, Frank Lloyd Wright Home and Studio Foundation

Frank Lloyd Wright's Home

(1889), Oak Park, Illinois

"Conceive now that an entire building might grow up out of conditions as a plant grows up out of soil, as free to be itself, to live its own life according to nature as is the tree. Dignified as a tree in the midst of nature."–1932

Wright created a harmonious relationship between his own home and its landscape through the use of natural materials and hues—brown cedar shingles and olive green trim that recall the site's plantings and the bark of surrounding mature trees. Reflecting the influence of the wooden Froebel blocks on young Wright, the house is a composition of primary, geometric shapes. The studio to the left of the home was added in 1898.

ABOVE: Orlando Giannini, mural in master bedroom, Wright's Oak Park home. This hand-painted mural depicts a stylized American Plains Indian, illustrating Wright's interest in Native American culture. RIGHT: Playroom, Oak Park home. Wright designed this barrel-vaulted space to inspire creativity in his six children. Bay windows on either side of the room extend the view beyond the wall plane and feature patterns of abstracted tulip flowers.

"Wood is universally beautiful to man. It is the most humanly intimate of all materials." —1928

LEFT: Dining room, Oak Park home. Wright created a sense of intimacy by surrounding the dining table with his signature tall-backed chairs and with a ceiling grille that cast warm, filtered light on the guests below. ABOVE: Frank Lloyd Wright, dining chair, designed for his Oak Park home, c. 1895, oak frame with leather seat, 57 1/2 × 18 × 19 1/2 inches. RIGHT: Restoration drawing of ceiling grille in dining room, c. 1977. The original, in wood, c. 1895, features a pattern of stylized leaves, branches, and acorns from an oak tree.

This bold, self-assured design was among the young Wright's first independent commissions and is considered a forerunner of the mature Prairie House.

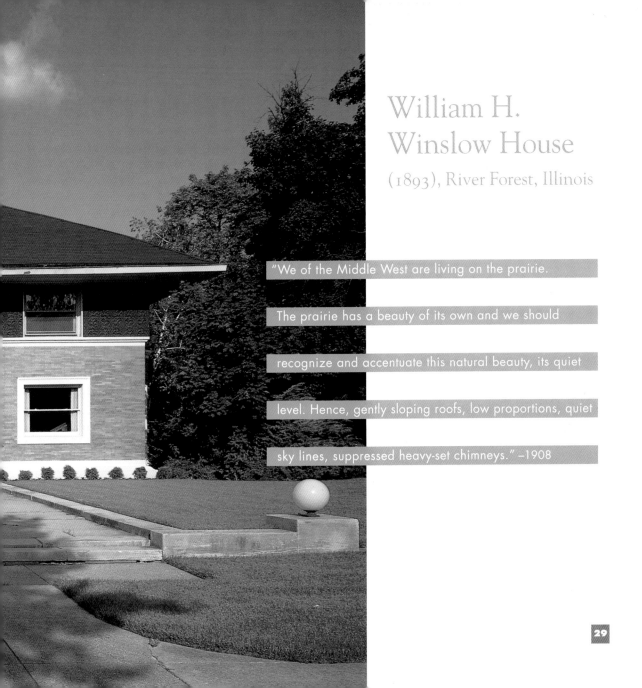

William H. Winslow House

(1893), River Forest, Illinois

"We of the Middle West are living on the prairie.

The prairie has a beauty of its own and we should

recognize and accentuate this natural beauty, its quiet

level. Hence, gently sloping roofs, low proportions, quiet

sky lines, suppressed heavy-set chimneys." –1908

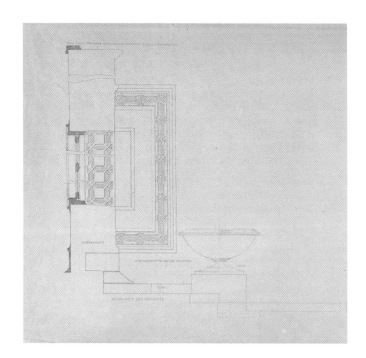

ABOVE AND RIGHT: William
H. Winslow Residence (1893).
Plate I, perspective view and detail,
from *Ausgeführte Bauten und
Entwürfe von Frank Lloyd Wright*
(The Wasmuth Portfolio), lithograph on cream wove paper,
25 ¼ × 16 inches. LEFT: The
home's broad eaves shadow a
plaster frieze with a foliate design
clearly influenced by Wright's
former employer, Louis Sullivan.

GEDRUCKT UND VERLEGT VON ERNST WASMUTH A.-G., BERLIN

Frank Lloyd Wright's Studio

(1898), Oak Park, Illinois

"Bring out the nature of the materials, let

their nature intimately into your scheme. . . .

Reveal the nature of the wood, plaster, brick,

or stone in your designs; they are all by

nature friendly and beautiful."–1908

The use of common brick, stone, and cedar linked this unusual building to its site and to Wright's adjacent home, but its sharp angles and bold shapes proclaimed to all passersby that this was no ordinary workplace.

LEFT: Entrance hall, Wright's Oak Park studio. The autumn shades in an intricate, art glass skylight transform this low, compressed space into a peaceful arbor, greeting visitors to the studio. RIGHT: Drafting room, Oak Park studio. Wright completed one quarter of his life's work in this dramatic, two-story atelier. A balcony is suspended by an ingenious system of chain harnesses, illustrating Wright's belief in the open expression of a building's structural elements.

LEFT: Passageway between Oak Park home and studio. Reluctant to destroy trees, Wright incorporated this one in his design, literally marrying the building and its natural surroundings. RIGHT: Library, Oak Park studio. Wright presented drawings to his clients in this dynamic space, composed of a series of stacked, rotated octagons.

Considered the first great Prairie House,
this dramatic residence is comprised of a
central mass with two symmetrical wings
and a carefully devised, pinwheel plan of
open, interlocking spaces.

Ward W. Willits House

(1901), Highland Park, Illinois

"The house began to associate

with the ground and become

natural to its prairie site." –1932

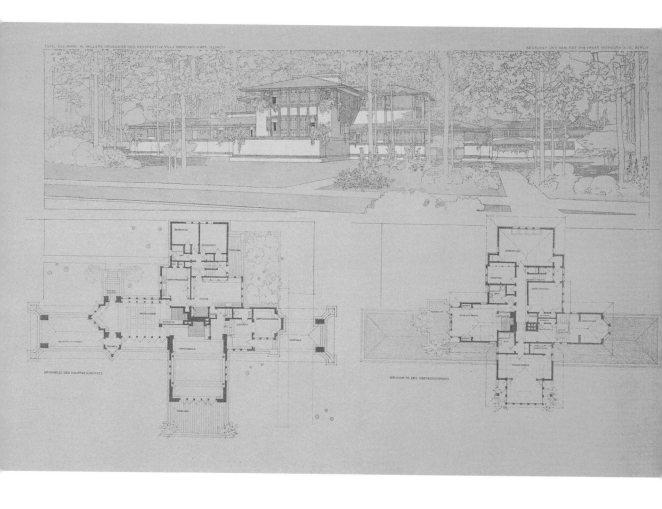

ABOVE: Ward W. Willits Residence (1901). Plate XXV
from *Ausgeführte Bauten und Entwürfe von Frank Lloyd
Wright* (The Wasmuth Portfolio), lithograph on cream wove
paper, 25¼ × 15 inches.   RIGHT: The staircase is topped
with an art glass skylight and a reproduction of one of
Wright's favorite sculptures, "Winged Victory." Wright
disapproved of classical ornament with the exception of
Greek sculpture, which he considered timeless.

Located down the street from Wright's own studio, this stately, el-shaped building was the first Prairie House in Oak Park. As in most Prairie houses, the living areas are located on the second level to afford the owner privacy, improved air circulation, and views of the outdoors. Wright despised basements and rarely incorporated them in his homes.

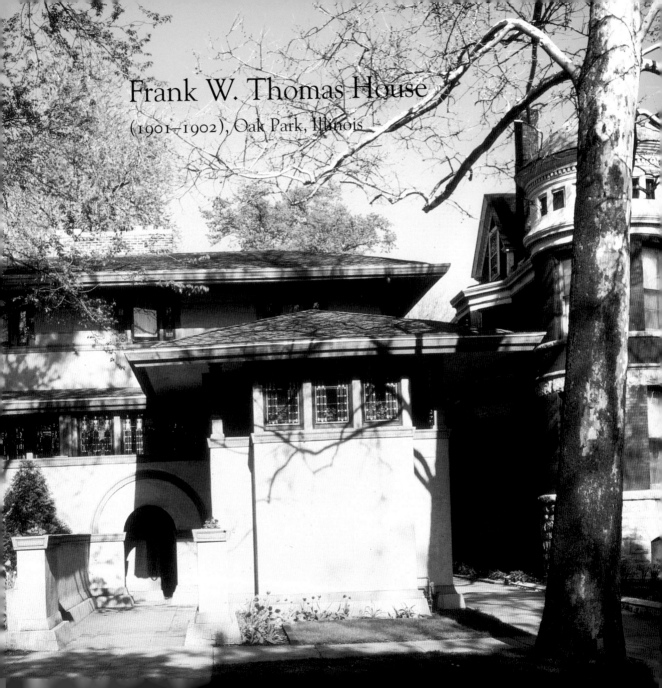

Frank W. Thomas House

(1901–1902), Oak Park, Illinois

ABOVE AND RIGHT: The art glass
windows and doors in this house are
among the most complex of Wright's
career, featuring opalescent glass and
gold leaf. The patterns in the glass and
in the beaded wood detail are stylized
versions of natural plant forms.

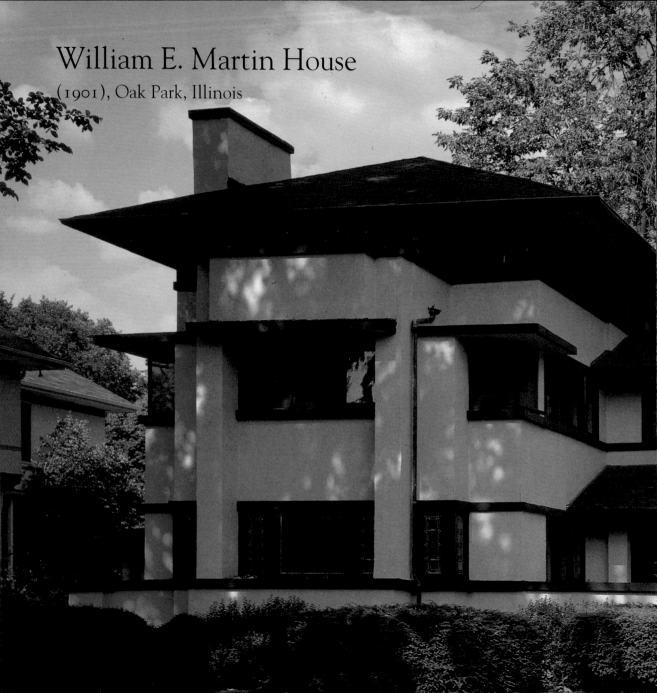

William E. Martin House

(1901), Oak Park, Illinois

This residence does not have the long, low silhouette typical of the Prairie Style, but through an anchoring porch extension, the gradual steps of the hipped roofs, and the use of wood banding, Wright created a three-story Prairie House.

"On Midwestern prairies I build, in three dimensions, houses that proclaim the prairie's quiet level. . . ." –1929

LEFT: Entry hall, William E. Martin House. Wright created wall openings to permit glimpses into adjacent rooms—a technique he favored in providing occupants with fresh vistas and a sense of discovery.
RIGHT: Dining room, William E. Martin House. Here, Wright replaced the traditional bay window with a triangular projection resembling the prow of a ship. He repeated this element in other buildings, including the Fricke and Robie houses.

William G. Fricke House

(1901), Oak Park, Illinois

Comprised of interlocking, cubic forms, the Fricke house foreshadows the strong geometric simplicity of Wright's later work. In contrast to the home's Prairie-Style detail is a dominant, three-story tower, which lends an imposing profile to the north façade.

The horizontal lines of this self-contained, rectangular building are emphasized through the use of narrow Roman brick, uninterrupted rows of art glass windows, and a low, wide chimney.

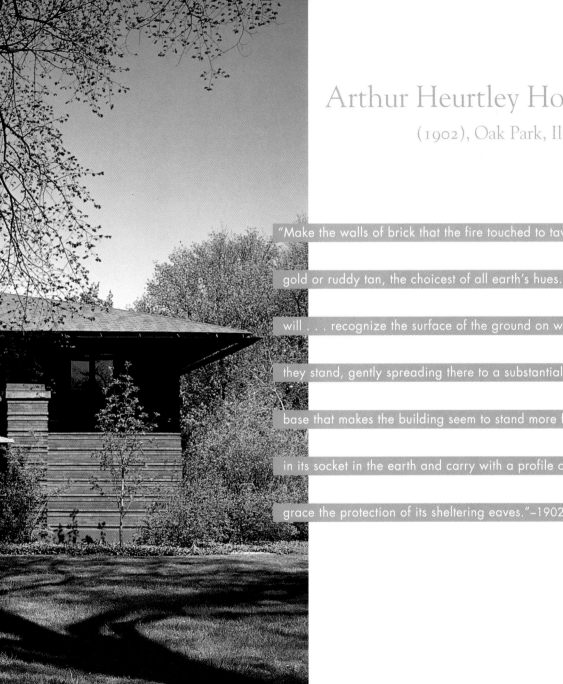

Arthur Heurtley House

(1902), Oak Park, Illinois

"Make the walls of brick that the fire touched to tawny

gold or ruddy tan, the choicest of all earth's hues. They

will . . . recognize the surface of the ground on which

they stand, gently spreading there to a substantial

base that makes the building seem to stand more firmly

in its socket in the earth and carry with a profile of

grace the protection of its sheltering eaves."–1902

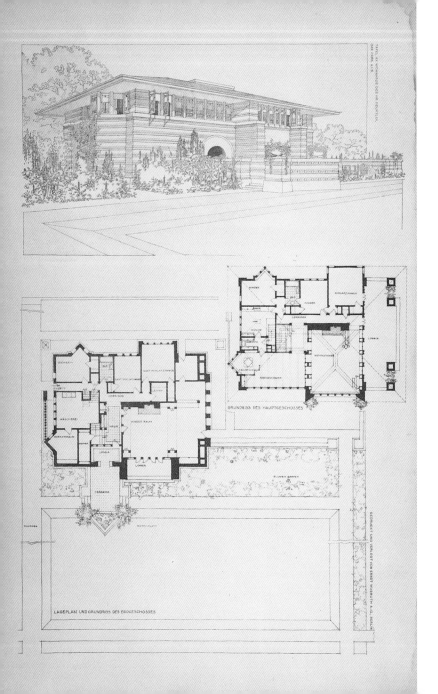

LEFT: Arthur Heurtley Residence (1902). Plate XX from *Ausgeführte Bauten und Entwürfe von Frank Lloyd Wright* (The Wasmuth Portfolio), lithograph on cream wove paper, 25 1/4 × 15 inches. RIGHT: Like many of Wright's Prairie houses, the Heurtley Residence features a hidden entrance, set back behind a gated archway. Evenly spaced, raised courses of Roman brick create texture and underline the home's long horizontal plan.

"To thus make of a dwelling place a complete work of art; in itself

as expressive and beautiful and more intimately related to life

than anything of detached sculpture or painting; lending itself

freely and suitably to the individual needs of the dwellers. . . ." –1910

The low, earth-hugging profile of this elaborate Prairie
House is perfectly suited to the flat, open terrain of
its Midwestern site. Client Susan Lawrence Dana
commissioned Wright to design not only the building—
which incorporated an earlier Italianate structure—but
also its rich collection of decorative arts, including
sculptures, murals, and complementary furnishings.

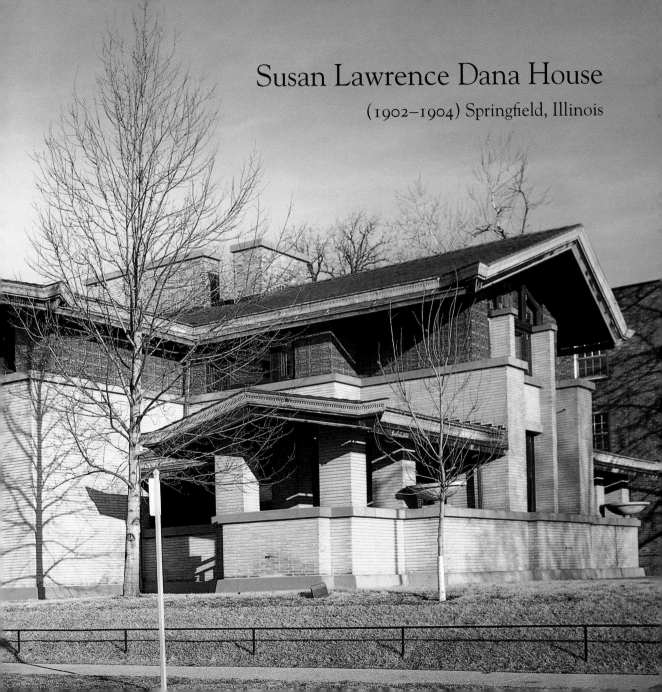

Susan Lawrence Dana House

(1902–1904) Springfield, Illinois

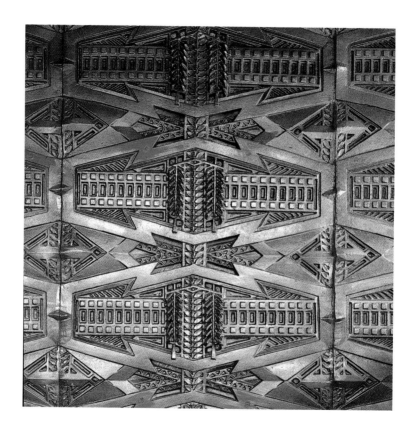

ABOVE: This decorative plaster frieze on
the exterior of the Dana House has been painted to imitate the appearance of aged copper.
RIGHT: Wright created the illusion of the
roof floating above the home's massive brick
piers by recessing a wall of casement windows
and exaggerating the overhang of the large,
triangular gable.

"These designs have grown as natural plants grow, the individuality of each is integral and as complete as skill, time, strength, and circumstance would permit." –1908

ABOVE: Wood banding applied to a barrel-vaulted ceiling draws the eye upward to the dining room's balcony and to its original murals by George Mann Niedecken. RIGHT: Wright disliked attics, preferring to utilize a building's upper space to create dramatic, two-story rooms for everyday living.

Peter A. Beachy House

(1906), Oak Park, Illinois

The gable and flared eaves of this residence illustrate the influence of Japanese culture on Wright, who traveled and worked in Japan and became an important collector of Japanese woodblock prints.

LEFT: In this open floor plan typical of the Prairie Style—conceived by Wright to encourage family interaction and activity—functional areas are defined by shifting ceiling heights and by geometric arrangements of wooden ceiling trim. ABOVE: A pergola extending to the south strengthens the link between the building's interior and its spacious natural site in the heart of the Frank Lloyd Wright Prairie School of Architecture Historic District.

Isabel Roberts House

(1908), River Forest, Illinois

LEFT: This Prairie Style home was designed for Isabel Roberts, who served as a bookkeeper and assisted with drafting in Wright's Oak Park studio. RIGHT: A two-story living room, highlighted by a wall of floor-to-ceiling leaded glass windows, gives this modestly sized residence a sense of grandeur.

Mrs. Thomas Gale House

(1909), Oak Park, Illinois

"The planes of the building parallel to the ground were all stressed . . . to grip the whole Earth. This parallel plane I called, from the beginning, the plane of the third dimension." –1932

More formal and geometric than Wright's
early Prairie houses, this structure is a
carefully ordered and balanced composition
of horizontal and vertical planes.

Frederick C. Robie House

(1909–1910), Chicago, Illinois

"A new sense of repose in flat planes and quiet 'streamline' effects had thereby and then found its way into building, as we can now see it admirably in steamships, airplanes, and motorcars." –1936

Wright embraced the principles of the machine age and used clean, geometric designs to create a technologically advanced building for his client, Frederick Robie, an entrepreneur and manufacturer of bicycles and automobile supplies. Wright took the sweeping horizontal lines characteristic of the Prairie House and stretched them to their limits in this strong, decisive design. Long bands of limestone trim, the use of Roman brick and radical cantilevers render the building a vivid symbol of shelter.

LEFT: Wright endeavored throughout his career to rid interiors of traditional partitions through the use of glass, partial walls, and open floor plans, clearly succeeding in this expansive, light-filled living space. RIGHT: The Robie House's extended overhangs, which define exterior porches as rooms, are made possible by concealed steel girders.

"My sense of wall was not the side of a box. It was

enclosure to afford protection against storm or heat

when this was needed. But it was also increasingly

to bring the outside world into the house, and let

the inside of the house go outside. In this sense I was

working toward the elimination of the wall as a

wall to reach the function of a screen. . . ."–1932

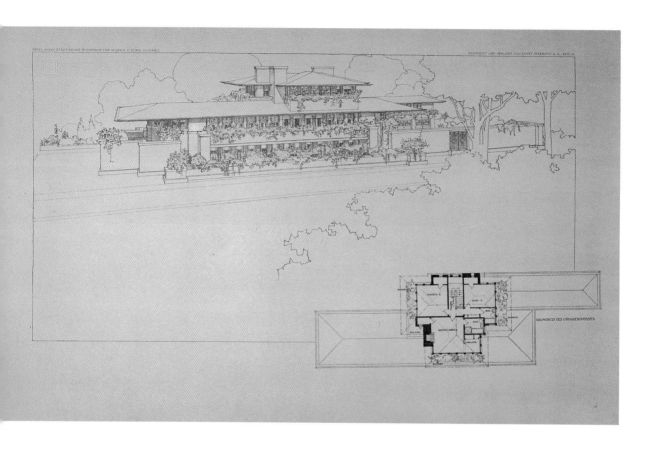

ABOVE: Frederick C. Robie House (1909–1910).
Plate XXXVII from *Ausgeführte Bauten und Entwürfe
von Frank Lloyd Wright* (The Wasmuth Portfolio),
lithograph on cream wove paper, 25¼ × 16 inches.
RIGHT: An entire wall of art glass casements
dissolves the boundary between the inside and outside
of the Robie House yet affords the occupants privacy
in their urban setting.

Frank Lloyd Wright, c. 1887.
RIGHT: Wright illustration for
The House Beautiful, c. 1896–1897,
collotype insert, 14 × 12 inches.

"The very strength of individuality
developed in a free nation . . . will
find expression in an art that is
indigenous . . . the hardy grace of the
wildflower perhaps rather than the
cultivated richness of the rose." –1900

SUGGESTED READING

Abernathy, Ann. *The Oak Park Home and Studio of Frank Lloyd Wright*. Oak Park, Illinois: Frank Lloyd Wright Home and Studio Foundation, 1988.

Birk, Melanie, editor. *Frank Lloyd Wright's Fifty Views of Japan*. San Francisco: Pomegranate Artbooks, 1996.

Brooks, H. Allen. *The Prairie School: Frank Lloyd Wright and His Midwest Contemporaries*. New York: W. W. Norton & Company, Inc. 1984.

Fields, Jeanette S. *Guidebook to the Architecture of River Forest*. River Forest, Illinois, 1990.

Futagawa, Yukio, ed. *Frank Lloyd Wright, Selected Houses, Volume 1*. Tokyo: A.D.A. Edita, 1991.

Hitchcock, Henry-Russell. *In the Nature of Materials: The Buildings of Frank Lloyd Wright 1887–1941*. New York: Da Capo Press, Inc., 1942.

Hoffmann, Donald. *Frank Lloyd Wright: Architecture and Nature*. New York: Dover Publications, Inc., 1986.

Hoffmann, Donald. *Frank Lloyd Wright's Robie House: The Illustrated Story of an Architectural Masterpiece*. New York: Dover Publications, Inc., 1984.

Manson, Grant Carpenter. *Frank Lloyd Wright to 1910: The First Golden Age*. New York: Von Nostrand Reinhold Company, 1958.

Pfeiffer, Bruce Brooks, ed. *The Collected Writings of Frank Lloyd Wright*, volumes 1 and 2. New York: Rizzoli, 1992.

Sprague, Paul. *Guide to Frank Lloyd Wright and Prairie School Architecture in Oak Park*. Village of Oak Park, Illinois, 1986.

Storrer, William Allin. *The Frank Lloyd Wright Companion*. Chicago: University of Chicago Press, 1993.

Twombly, Robert. *Frank Lloyd Wright: His Life and Architecture*. New York: Wiley, 1979.

Wright, Frank Lloyd. *An Autobiography*. New York: Longmans, Green and Company, 1932.

Wright, Frank Lloyd. *Drawings and Plans of Frank Lloyd Wright, The Early Period (1893–1909)*. New York: Dover Publications, 1983. (Republication of *Ausgeführte Bauten und Entwürfe von Frank Lloyd Wright*.)

Wright, John Lloyd. *My Father Frank Lloyd Wright*. New York: Dover Publications, 1992.

A NOTE TO READERS

Three National Historic Landmarks discussed in this book—the Frank Lloyd Wright Home and Studio, the Susan Lawrence Dana House (currently known as the Dana-Thomas House), and the Frederick C. Robie House—are open to the public as museums, enabling visitors to experience Wright's work firsthand and to witness the genesis, growth and mature expression of the Prairie House.

For more information contact:

The Frank Lloyd Wright
Home and Studio
951 Chicago Avenue
Oak Park, Illinois 60302
708-848-1976

Information is also available on walking tours of the surrounding Frank Lloyd Wright Prairie School of Architecture National Historic District, as well as an annual open-house tour, "Wright Plus."

The Frederick C. Robie House
5757 South Woodlawn Avenue
Chicago, Illinois 60637
708-848-1976

The Dana-Thomas House
301 East Lawrence Avenue
Springfield, Illinois 62703
217-782-6776

NOTES

1   Frank Lloyd Wright, *Ausgeführte Bauten und Entwürfe von Frank Lloyd Wright* ("Wasmuth Portfolio") (Berlin: Ernst Wasmuth, 1910), introduction.
2   Frank Lloyd Wright, *An Autobiography* (New York: Longmans, Green and Company, 1932), p. 3.
3   *An Autobiography*, p. 1
4   *An Autobiography*, p. 137.
5   Grant Carpenter Manson, *Frank Lloyd Wright to 1910: The First Golden Age* (New York: Von Nostrand Reinhold Company, 1958), p. 68.
6   Frederick Gutheim, Editor, *Frank Lloyd Wright on Architecture, Selected Writings 1894–1940* (New York: Duell, Sloan and Pearce, 1941), p. 34.
7   *An Autobiography*, p. 145.
8   *An Autobiography*, p. 140.
9   John Lloyd Wright, *My Father Frank Lloyd Wright* (New York: Dover Publications, Inc. 1992), p. 35.
10 *An Autobiography*, p. 139.
11 Frank Lloyd Wright, *The Japanese Print: An Interpretation* (New York: Horizon Press/The Frank Lloyd Wright Foundation, 1967), p. 20.
12 *Frank Lloyd Wright on Architecture, Selected Writings 1894–1940*, p. 141.
13 Frank Lloyd Wright, *Ausgeführte Bauten und Entwürfe von Frank Lloyd Wright*, introduction.

Quotes on pages 22, 39, 60, 65, 68, and 73 were excerpted from *An Autobiography*.
Quotes on the back cover and pages 1, 26, 29, 32, 48, 53, 71, and 77 were excerpted from *Frank Lloyd Wright on Architecture, Selected Writings 1894–1940*.
Quote on page 56 was excerpted from *Ausgeführte Bauten und Entwürfe von Frank Lloyd Wright*.